Snippets of Billy Connolly

Dave Farnham

ISBN: 150231181X
ISBN-13: 978-1502311818

DISCLAIMER

While every effort has been made to ensure the
information in this book is correct, human error is always a
possibility and therefore the author cannot accept
responsibility for any inaccuracies.

CONTENTS

INTRODUCTION

For over forty years, Billy Connolly has been amusing, entertaining and scandalising the public with his wit, music and acting talent. His broad Glaswegian accent, a notable trademark, far from holding him back has contributed to his wide appeal. His humour is often of the x-rated variety – he fearlessly says out loud what others only think – but is perceptive and funny even when it shocks. His appearance, with his long, somewhat unruly hair and his goatee beard (which disappeared for a time in the early nineties), makes him one of the most instantly recognisable personalities on the television and cinema screens.

In a Channel 4 programme on the 'top 100 stand-up comedians', he came top, no mean achievement for someone with such a disadvantaged start in life.

His early career (after being a shipyard boilermaker) was as a folk-singer in a moderately successful group The Humblebums, alongside Gerry Rafferty who later achieved fame with his hit 'Baker Street". It was Billy's tendency to tell increasingly longer jokes between songs that led to the breakup of the band but which also pointed him in the direction of a career in comedy.

Since those days in the early seventies Billy Connolly has been a household name: his talents, in addition to his music and comedy, have included serious acting, writing and fundraising. And as if that isn't enough, he's also an accomplished, exhibited artist.

His wife Pamela, once a familiar comedienne in her own right as well as later achieving prominence as a therapist, has been his constant support, biographer and soulmate and is a very significant part of the story of the complex, multi-faceted personality that is Billy Connolly.

This book brings together quotes from Billy himself as well as from others speaking about him. It seeks to inform and entertain and shed light on a man who has become a British, as well as Scottish, institution.

BIO FOR BILLY CONNOLLY

Nickname: The Big Yin (The Big One)

1942 November 24th, Born in Glasgow. Named after his father, William Connolly, who was in the Army. His mother, Mary, was a hospital canteen worker. He had an older sister, Florence.

1946 Mary abandoned her children while her husband was still away with the Army. William's sisters reluctantly took Billy and Florence in to live with them but ill-treated them.

1957 Left school, 15 years old, and became bread delivery boy, later joining a shipyard as a boilermaker. Also joined the Territorial Army.

1960s Taught himself to play the banjo and took up folk singing. Formed a folk duo, The Humblebums, with Tam Harvey. They recorded one album. Harvey left and Jerry Rafferty (later of 'Baker Street' fame) took over, the pair recording two albums for Transatlantic Records, which found success in a niche market. Connolly became popular at live gigs because of his jokes between songs.

1969   Maried Iris Pressagh, with whom he had two children.

1971 The Humblebums broke up in 1971. Connolly was encouraged by the head of Transatlantic to develop his skills as a comedian.

1972 Released his first comedy album *Billy Connolly Live*.

1974   Released his second album, *Solo Concert* an immediate success, though because of the nature of its content it was banned by many radio stations. In 1975, Connolly appeared on the Michael Parkinson Show, the first of fifteen appearances on that show and found overnight stardom. He was befriended by Elton John, who took him to America as a warm-up act. This was not a success, the Americans being unable to understand his Glaswegian accent.   Back in the UK, however, his popularity continued to grow, particularly through his records – a mixture of comedy and songs.

During the 1970s he and his wife became increasingly alcohol-dependent.

In 1978 he had a part in the film *Absolution*. In 1979 he joined the cast of *The Secret Policeman's Ball*, a fundraising show on behalf of Amnesty International which also starred John Cleese, Michael Palin, Rowan Atkinson and Peter Cook. It was also in 1979 that he first met Pamela Stephenson, comedienne of *Not The Nine O'Clock* News fame, later to become his wife.

1981 Appeared in *The Secret Policeman's Other Ball*, which was filmed. The film was particularly popular in the USA, partly because of the American love for the Pythons, Connolly gaining a receptive audience there on the back of this success.

1981 Left his wife and started living with Pamela Stephenson.

1984 December 31st, he became teetotal.

1985 Divorced his wife Iris.

1987 Undertook his first world tour.

1989 His father died following a stroke.

1989 Married Pamela Stephenson in Fiji. They have three daughters.

1990 Appeared on US television with Whoopie Goldberg, which was a huge success, making him a star in America.

1991 He and Pamela moved to Hollywood.

1993 His mother, whom he last saw in 1972, died of motor neurone disease.

1990s During this decade he made numerous live stage and TV appearances as well as playing film roles, notably in *Mrs Brown*, where he appeared alongside Judi Dench and which gained him a BAFTA nomination.

2000s Continued success as a film actor and comedian.

2001 *Billy*, Pamela Stephenson's first biographical book about him, was published, revealing for the first time the sexual abuse he suffered at the hands of his father.

2001 Awarded honorary doctorate by Glasgow University

2003 Awarded CBE in Queen's Birthday Honours. Also gained BAFTA Lifetime Achievement award.

2006 Awarded honorary doctorate by Royal Scottish Academy of Music and Drama.

2010 Awarded honorary doctorate by Nottingham Trent University. Also became Freeman of the City of Glasgow.

2011 Filmed ITV documentary, *Billy Connolly's Route 66*, during which his motor bike went out of control and fell on him, breaking a rib. He continued filming the following week.

2012 Received BAFTA Scotland award for outstanding achievement in television and film.

2012 Starred in Dustin Hoffman's film *Quartet*.

2013 Had surgery for prostate cancer. He also revealed that he was being treated for early symptoms of Parkinson's disease.

2014 Filming for part 2 of *The Hobbit*, in which he plays a warrior dwarf.

ABOUT HIMSELF

How he acquired his nickname, 'The Big Yin':

"My father was a very strong man. Broad and strong. He had an 18½ inch neck collar, huge like a bull. He was 'Big Billy' and I was 'wee Billy'. And then I got bigger than him and the whole thing got out of control. And then I became The Big Yin in Scotland. So we'd go into the pub and someone would say, 'Billy Connolly was in'. 'Oh, Big Billy or wee billy?' 'The Big Yin' 'Oh, wee Billy'. If you were a stranger you'd think, 'What are these people talking about.'"

*

"I think my securities far outweigh my insecurities. I am not nearly as afraid of myself and my imagination as I used to be."

*

DAVE FARNHAM

He found it hard to 'pick up' women:

"I never knew when to make a move. I'd end up laughing
with them all night and find out we'd become friends,
which I didn't particularly want. I mean, I had lots of
friends already."

*

"I don't aim to offend."

*

"I have been made redundant before and it is a terrible
blow; redundant is a rotten word because it makes you
think you are useless."

*

I've been a poser for f***ing years. I say, pose your arse
off. You know, have a laugh."

*

"I'm famous for my bottom dances, but you'll only see my
bum and willy if you raise a million pounds within an
hour."

8

*

"A lot of people say that it's a lack of vocabulary that makes you swear. Rubbish. I know thousands of words but I still prefer 'f***.'"

*

When asked how he felt about being on his wife's couch (Pamela Stephenson is a psychologist) he said, laughing:

'Oh, I loved it,' (laughs) 'I'm a work in progress, me.'

*

After he gave up alcohol:

I felt fitter and I thought I was better on stage after I'd stopped drinking. So I started doing other things, too. I stopped smoking and I stopped eating meat. And all of a sudden I became this other guy. I disappeared. I had this 30-inch waist. I have a picture at home and I have a leather suit on and my face is all sunk in, and I look like a cadaver. I thought, "God! Eat something! Chew something!" And I've just gradually got back to my own shape. But it's a good thing to know you can change.'

*

Billy Connolly was at home in New York in 2013, with his wife, Pamela Stephenson, when his oncologist phoned to tell him that a health check had shown that he had prostate cancer. Also during that day, he found out that he had Parkinson's disease.

"It was a funny week. On the Monday I got hearing aids. On the Tuesday I got pills for heartburn, which I have to take all the time. And on the Wednesday I got news that I had prostate cancer and Parkinson's disease,"

*

He spoke in a radio interview, in the USA, about how he first discovered he had prostate cancer (for which, after surgery, he was given the all clear in December 2013.)

"It was the strangest thing of all. I was doing Conan O'Brien's thing and they put me up in the Sportsmen's Lodge in Los Angeles. I was walking through the lobby and every time I had gone through there was a crowd of boys and girls and a couple of adults. It turned out they were dancers from Australia. The guy who was in charge of them came over to me one day and said 'Billy, I'm a big fan, I'm from Tasmania'.He said, 'I'm a surgeon and I have been watching you walking, you have a strange gait'. That was the way he put it. He said 'You're showing distinct signs of early onset Parkinson's disease, see your doctor'. I think it was the way I held myself when I was walking. Then they did blood tests and various other little bits and pieces and told me I had it.'

*

He spoke about his diagnosis of prostate cancer:

"It was found by the routine finger up the bum test. When I was told by the doctor I had cancer I said to him, 'I've never been told that before'. Usually you are only told once. The doctor in the hospital, the one who operated on me, said to me 'the good news is you're not going to die'. I said that it never crossed my mind that I might. It's that arrogance thing, I think I'm going to live forever."

*

About his Parkinson's disease:

'I prefer not to give it any notice. I don't see much shaking going on and I have always had a sh** memory anyway.

"I have forgotten things my entire career. I was taking drugs to control the Parkinson's but I'm not on them anymore. The doctor said the side effects were stronger than the effects. I never noticed any side effects but he told me they could include a deep interest in sex and gambling."

*

"It's my mind, and I reserve the right to change it as often as I like."

*

I'm actually pale blue: it takes me a week of sunbathing to turn white."

*

"I worry about ridiculous things, you know, how does a guy who drives a snowplough get to work in the morning... that can keep me awake for days."

*

"I always look skint. When I buy a Big Issue, people take it out of my hand and give me a pound."

*

"There comes a point when you don't give a sh** what anybody thinks. It doesn't happen all at once, but it's lovely when it does. Criticism used to worry me before, but I can suddenly write it off. It's too late. I don't have the time to spend thinking about it anymore. I need that time to live with."

*

"I was always confused with what was near-sight and what was far-sight. Now I'm not confused at all: I've got both, I don't give a f*** which is which."

*

"I'd always been scared of people with tertiary education and high intellects in case they found me wanting. I thought they viewed me as just a welder who knew a few jokes."

*

"I'm okay. I'm old and I'm cold. I'm going deaf, I can't walk very well. (laughs) I'm getting a lot better, I'm a lot better than I was, which is a wonderful position to be in. Someone once said growing old is not for sissies, they knew what they were talking about."

*

"I'm now a Doctor of Letters. Most of them Fs and Bs."

*

"I have made myself very windswept and interesting, as the years have gone on. Because I was born a sort of fart. So I've tried everything to be exotic. I've fought being plain all my life, but it keeps coming back."

*

"I always look... when I buy something expensive, I look as if I stole it, you know. There's a look about me, y'know."

*

"I'm a shoe-y person — my all-time favourites are cowboy boots with the devil getting married."

*

"I've also always loved flashy socks. It's not because I want to show off. I'm just not beige.'

ABOUT LIFE AND PEOPLE

"Life for me is great. I'm a very f***in' wealthy person, I'm married to a very beautiful woman and I get laid with monotonous regularity."

*

"I think of my life as a series of moments and I've found that the great moments often don't have too much to them. They're not huge, complicated events; they're just magical wee moments when somebody says 'I love you' or 'You're a really good at what you do' or simply 'You're a good person'."

*

'Life is a waste of time and time is a waste of life. Get wasted all the time and you'll have the time of your life!'

*

"Life is supposed to be fun. It's not a job or occupation. We're here only once and we should have a bit of a laugh."

*

"When people say "life is short". What the f***? Life is the longest damn thing anyone ever f***ing does! What can you do that's longer?"

*

"If you don't know how to meditate at least try to spend some time every day just sitting."

*

"I'm a citizen of the world. I like it that way. The world's a wonderful. I just think that some people are pretty badly represented. But when you speak to the people themselves they're delightful. They all want so little."

*

"Never turn down an opportunity to shout 'F*** them all!' at the top of your voice."

*

"Heckling is an act of cowardice. If you want to speak, get up in front of the microphone and speak, don't sit in the dark hiding. It's easy to hide and shout and waste people's time."

*

"Before you judge a man, walk a mile in his shoes. After that who cares?... He's a mile away and you've got his shoes!"

*

"What always staggers me is that when people blow their noses, they always look into their hankies to see what came out. What do they expect to find?"

*

"If you give people a chance, they shine."

*

"Gerry Rafferty was a hugely talented songwriter and

singer who will be greatly missed. I was privileged to have spent my formative years working with Gerry and there remained a strong bond of friendship between us that lasted until his untimely death. Gerry had extraordinary gifts and his premature passing deprives the world of a true genius."

*

About his wife, Pamela:

"With Pam, I discovered that you could not get away with anything. Could not get away from her intelligence. There were always so many whys going on. And I thought, Oh God , you know. I had to own up to everything, which no one had ever asked me to do before."

"I'd always been open to change, and she showed me how I might go about that."

ABOUT MARRIAGE AND SEX

"Marriage is a wonderful invention: then again, so is a
bicycle repair kit."

*

"Let a person remain themselves. There is an attitude that
when you are married you have to become this one thing
and stop being two people. There is nothing weird about
going fishing — let him go fishing. There is nothing weird
about ballroom dancing — let her dance. Just because guys
are doing tango with your wife doesn't mean they are a
threat — let her go."

*

"To keep the fire burning brightly there's one easy rule:
Keep the two logs together, near enough to keep each
other warm and far enough apart-about a finger's breadth-

for breathing room. Good fire, good marriage, same rule."

*

"I've started touching my willy. It is one of my more disconcerting traits recently. Because I've been talking about people who touch theirs, and it has led me to touch mine. And there's a strange comfort to be had. You don't wiggle about or anything. You check it like you check your change, or credit card or ... willy. I think maybe it's gonna fall off, when you get older, like your hair. Perhaps when you're older, you lose your willy. Panic in your soul. Usually happens to men in their thirties. Happened to me in mine. You're lying in your bath, luxuriating. And you look down. And there's your first grey pubic hair. That's your starter for ten. And I thought 'God, how awful. Nobody told me about that.' Cause you don't get like Grecian 2000 adverts, where the guy... put a great wallop of it down the front of the jeans."

*

"I have been kind of obsessed with sex, as well, you see. It took me an extraordinary length of time to loose my virginity. Oh God almighty, it was ages."

*

"Apparently, women need to feel loved to have sex, and men need to have sex to feel loved, so the basic act of continuing the species requires a lie from one of you."

*

"If women are so bloody perfect at multitasking, how come they can't have a headache and sex at the same time?"

*

"A gypsy girl sent an email to an agony Aunt 'I am 12 years old and haven't had sex yet, do you think my brother is queer?'"

*

"American sex shops are the most bizarre. They sell these inflatable dolls, but they also sell just the head -- supposedly for people to drive along the highway with."

ON GROWING OLD

"Waking up and getting out of bed is quite a painful thing sometimes. But you mustn't give in, you mustn't act your age."

*

"When I go home to Glasgow and I meet people I went to school with. Some of them are in great shape but some of them have voluntarily become old men. They've gone for the old-guy haircut and the old-guy sports jacket and that terrifying little half a raincoat they wear."

*

"There's school and jail. Old folks' homes are all pretty much the same. I'm against them. There's a mindset of getting rid of the old because they're old."

*

"Fall in love and fancy people. Stay attractive to your partner and have sex – don't give it up."

*

"Accept old age but keep loving your music, keep loving your poetry, keep loving Dylan, keep loving The Beatles."

*

About the retired opera singers & musicians who had supporting roles in 'Quartet':

"That was one of the best parts of the film. They were real musicians and they played all the time like real musicians do. You can't stop them, between takes you felt them playing. And they hadn't had a phone call in 20 years, most of them. They were all lead players, ace players, but they hadn't been asked to work because of their age, which is really weird."

*

"Don't go for the old baggy-arse trousers and the f***ing beige shirt. And don't go for this dressing the same as your wife."

*

"Wear sturdy socks, learn to grow out of medium underwear and, if you must lie about your age, do it in the other direction. Tell people you're ninety-seven and they'll think you look f***ing great."

*

About how the make-up department worked on his appearance in Quartet:

"As you notice I'm not very wrinkly and I have this going on," (Connolly pointed to his white hair & goatee beard). "But they thought they could make me look older and they did. They cut my hair and aged me up a little."

*

"I think disgraceful is the way to do it. Be a nuisance, stay alive. In this bit of the world especially, not so much in America, but in Britain you're encouraged to wear a cardie and have the crotch of your trousers away down at your knees – bum fainters they call it in Scotland, because if you look at it from behind it looks as if your bum's fainted"

*

"You're constantly told to grow up. 'Grow up, it's time

you grew up, you've got some growing up to do boy'. What they really mean is, get boring, stop being angry, stop being interesting, stop being a nuisance. I would say don't grow up. By all means grow old, but don't grow up. Don't be beige."

*

"I'm starting to have problems with remembering things but who doesn't when they get to my age. You definitely can't refer to me as a spring chick any more.

"I get blanks all the time now, the curtains fall down in front of your eyes so you just keep talking till you remember your material that you were going to say.

"When you're nervous, you forget everything you were supposed to do and you just think, 'What am I going to say to these people?'

"And when you go out, you become the other guy. Sometimes you get blanks, just like jetlag. I'm not getting any younger.

"It's something that comes with age. I've had a pretty good run of it, to get to me 70s and still be standing upright is half the battle. You just take it all as it comes, don't you?"

*

About when he dies:

"I don't think I want a resting place. I want to be scattered to the wind."

"I've said a lot of things about my own funeral, but it's all bulls**t. Horses and Vikings and burning ships and all that. Actually, I'd like to think we could have the coffin in a hearse, empty. And the real me being buried somewhere by pals, quietly, with a tree on top of me."

ON FILMS & TV

"I'd never consciously left home to see a zombie movie. They were fine by me, but I had no intention of ever being in one. But I've been learning more about it as I've been doing interviews. I didn't even know there were specialist zombie magazines and clubs. I heard the other day that a radio station had asked people if they'd made preparations for an attack by zombies, and a staggering number of people replied yes!"

*

"Without arts programmes there's only reality TV, and reality TV needs the arts to show it what reality is."

*

"I hate those earnest TV documentaries that are the world according to people with glasses who know better than you."

∗

"I'm a huge film star... but you have to hurry to the movies, because I usually die in the first fifteen f***ing minutes. I'm the only guy I know who died in a f***ing Muppet movie."

∗

"A thing I haven't noticed in England, which is a very, very good thing - that is, a good thing you haven't got it. It's in Scotland they say 'Well that's all from television tonight. I bid you all a very, very good night, and especially those of you who live alone.' He has just reminded them. Some of them are terrifying, they say 'And those of you, who live alone, don't forget to lock all... lock the windows.' And stuff like that."

∗

"It's a very modern thing, that dependence on youth. If you get old black and white movies, those movies in the Forties, movies were all full of old people. There were hardly any young people. The young people were played by people in their 30s or 40s. The young crumpet would be 35 or 38, mincing around.

"There was a change in the 1950s. I think they invented the teenager in the 1950s, there was no such thing before that, and they stuck them in everywhere they could.

"I hope they just get back to the way they did before, or a mixture of the both, and use older actors instead of having the token old one, like Driving Miss Daisy, every now and again. Have it the way life is, a mixture."

*

About the popular BBC 1 'Strictly Come Dancing:

"They did ask me to do 'Strictly' and I straight out said, 'No.'

"I don't know, there's this massive pressure with a show like that, I don't think I'd want to join something like that.

"Although they can ask me in a few years, I might have changed my mind at that point."

ABOUT OTHER COUNTRIES

"I've always wanted to go to Switzerland to see what the
army does with those wee red knives."

*

"I love Los Angeles. It reinvents itself every two days."

*

"I loved Japan. I used to read a lot about it when I was a
child. And I always wanted to go. And it was delightful. I
absolutely loved it. What a smashing place."

*

"This country is in a terrible state, according to some people, and I know why. Now you'd blamed it on lot of things, on all unemployment and the value of the pound and all sorts of other magic things. It's because the national anthem is boring. No, no, don't get me wrong, I'm not arguing with the lyrics. Well, I am. But not them all. I mean, I think the Queen should be saved, I think it's a great idea. And if anybody is gonna save her, God is the very chap. Who am I to rock the boat? Not I, nice person, showbusiness personality. It's an appalling song, and it's racist, and it's anti-Scottish. The fourth verse is all about Marshal Wade coming up, to give us a belt in the mouth. And I don't like it. 'And with a mighty rush, rebellious Scots to crush.' Oh, do you bloody think so? I don't see any rush to Hamden to crush anybody. I rest my case."

*

On a visit to Ireland:

"I've always liked it here. Part of me is Irish… my family comes from the west coast, so whenever I come to Ireland I get a wee tingling in my heart that I'm where I belong."

*

About America:

"I love the positive attitude to life there, the optimism. It's an attitude that can't be bought. Britain is negative, it's full of s***heads, class system and religious bigots."

*

"It's not just Scotland, it's all of Britain: this negativity. You can see it in the obsession with so-called reality TV. It's donkeys watching f***ing donkeys. It's full of people who think you get bright by going to a gym. You know, we seem to have become a country where the highest ambition is to become a f***ing television presenter or, worse, a children's television presenter. People who know so much about children that they think they like being shouted at. All those ninnies! Autocue comedians, wearing glasses to look intelligent. I hate it, loathe it."

*

"I left Scotland because it was time for me to leave in millions of ways. I outgrew it, or at least I outgrew the media. It was becoming very uncomfortable for me. The negativity there felt like a disease, you know."

*

Speaking to Ireland's 'TV Now' magazine:

"I've been having a great year, the time of my life. The Hobbit was a dream job to get.
"I love travel and getting to stay down in New Zealand, playing this warrior dwarf with a red Mohawk and hair down to my arse.

"It's been wonderful... It's like being back at school with those lads, like you're on a class trip."

DAVE FARNHAM

ABOUT THE WEATHER AND FOOTBALL

"There are two seasons in Scotland: June and Winter."

*

"In Scotland, there is no such thing as bad weather - only the wrong clothes."

*

"I hate all those weathermen, too, who tell you that rain is bad weather. There's no such thing as bad weather, just the wrong clothing, so get yourself a sexy raincoat and live a little. "

*

"Scotland has the only football team in the world that does a lap of disgrace."

*

Billy Connolly joked that for years he thought that one club's name was "Partick Thistle Nil."

*

About the manager of the Scotland World Cup team in 1978:

"Ally MacLeod thinks that tactics are a new kind of mint."

ON ART, MUSIC AND ROYALTY

"I still do my comedy and my performance stuff and my acting so it's not all-consuming. But I do find myself drawing more and more these days."

*

"I don't understand art-speak. My pictures are big doodles. I'm amazed what people come up with when they look at them. There's one of a figure with two heads that somebody thought must be a comment on the state of matrimony. None of it is a comment on anything."

*

"Art, for me, bears no relation to comedy or music. My art is pure and 'unjudged'. I am creating it for myself – it is personal and private whereas with a film, comedy show or music you expect people to be critiquing, watching, assessing. Art is different; it liberates you."

*

"I like Dali and Magritte. I also like the Scottish artist John Byrne, another surrealist."

*

I used to be a folk singer, but I was... dreadful. I had a voice like a goose farting in the fog.

*

"The only time I would like to see was the 20s and 30s in America because I love the music and the style and the optimism, I wanted to see New York being built. I wanted to see all that, you know."

*

Referring to Prince Charles:

"I think if he were king, he would be a jolly, casual sort of king."

*

About Princess Anne

"She looks like a horse just s*** into her handbag."

ON COMEDY AND FAME

"It's very awkward to be kind of big in your own field. It limits what you're offered. People are swayed by the fact that you're a comedian or a musician or whatever they think you are. When it comes to choosing you, they get a bit shaky about offering you a different type of role. But I've really been very lucky. When you compare me to other comedians, I've been very fortunate. So you'll get no complaints."

*

In 1976 when Billy Connolly supported Elton John in a series of concerts at Madison Square Garden, the reaction to him was hostile:

"It was cruel and uncalled for. People often say that about comedians: 'He had his corners knocked off...' So it encourages a*******s to boo you everywhere you go. But some p***k singing *My Way* gets away with murder!"

*

"I've always been fascinated by the difference between the jokes you can tell your friends but you can't tell to an audience. There's a fine line you have to tread because you don't know who is out there in the auditorium. A lot of people are too easily offended."

*

"I don't have wild dogs chasing people with scripts away from my door. I get my share. I've done okay. But I usually do independent stuff because that's mostly what I'm offered."

*

"As soon as I got successful, the Scottish press started picking on me. It's something they reserve just for me."

*

"Don't tell me how to do my job. I don't come to your workplace and tell you how to sweep up."

*

"Fame is being asked to sign your autograph on the back of a cigarette packet."

*

"Once you become successful, people know where you live, the type of house you live in, the kind of car you drive, the clothes you wear, and so it would be patronising to go and talk like a welder. Welding's a mystery to me now. You can't go back, your life changes every day."

*

"And as a comedian, working with other comedians, when you work with good ones, or musicians, it makes you good."

*

He was concerned initially about being in the film 'Quartet' with Maggie Smith, Tom Courtenay and Pauline Collins:

"Before I did it I thought, 'Oh my God, I can't act with them, they'll be acting all over me and I'll be standing like a fool not knowing what to do', but it wasn't like that."

*

"Dustin (Hoffmann, directed the film ('Quartet') gave us loads and loads of freedom. Not only that, we would do these 12, 14-hour days, like you do when you're filming, and then he would go off and work at night on the script. Then he'd come back in the morning looking a little tired but behaving like 100 per cent, having changed a lot of things. It kept the whole thing alive and well."

ON RELIGION

"Religion is a real growth industry in Scotland. The BBC religious department has got 14 offices. What do they do all day? You can't hear the typewriters for the rattling of the rosaries, up there. It's very odd, and you get this never ending procession of wee men who come on at night, and tell you how dreadful the world is. And then in the most patronising possible way, try to introduce you to God. No, if there is a god, and I suppose there is, really. 'Cause I've always thought, if you believe in God, if anybody believes in God, there is one, you know, and it's not up for question."

*

"When I was a kid I used to pray every night for a new bike. Then I realised that the Lord doesn't work that way, so I stole a bike and asked him to forgive me."

*

"I was brought up as a Catholic. I've got A-level guilt."

*

"A lot of people are too easily offended. Religious people, for instance. They've been offending other people for centuries."

*

"If Jesus was a Jew, how come he has a Mexican first name?"

*

"I don't believe in angels, no. But I do have a wee parking angel. It's on my dashboard and you wind it up. The wings flap and it's supposed to give you a parking space. It's worked so far."

*

"It seems to me that Islam and Christianity and Judaism all have the same god, and he's telling them all different things."

*

"I don't believe in angels and I have trouble with the whole God thing. I don't want to say I don't believe in God, but I don't think I do. But I believe in people who do."

*

"53 f***ing virgins! The very thought of 53 f***ing virgins, it's a nightmare! It's not a f***ing present, it's not a prize- it's a punishment! Give me 2 fire-breathing whores any day of the week. I'm a slut, man!"

*

"The religion in Scotland is one of the most patronising things... after the weather."

ABOUT WAR & TERRORISM

"What horrifies me most about war memorials is that no anti-war sentiments are ever displayed. It's as if war is fun or noble, when actually it's all about sh** and snot and blood and guts and soldiers stomachs hanging out and people with their faces blown off. But they never showed that side of it. Perhaps, if they did, there'd be less of it.

"I remember seeing a picture of a soldier in Vietnam who was sitting, waiting to die, with his jaw missing. His head now started at the top row of teeth; everything beneath that was gone. They didn't put that on the recruitment posters, did they? But that's what war is to me. And I don't care who we're fighting, I don't hate them enough to do something like that to them."

*

"I've had it with terrorists of all colours and f***ing descriptions. F***ing bringing terror to some innocent person's life. F*** you. Osama Bin Laden lives in a cave, sh**s in a f***ing bucket. Why are we scared of this p***k? F*** you, Bin Laden!"

*

"The great thing about Glasgow is that if there's a nuclear attack it'll look exactly the same afterwards."

ABOUT POLITICS & POLITICIANS

"Do you remember that politician who died with the
fishnet tights and all that? Aw, his poor family. I wonder
how they dress him in the coffin?"

*

"That man (Ronald Reagan), he sits at that desk in the
White House, and the button is there that can end the
world: BOOM! My father's younger than him and we don't
give him the controls for the television!"

*

"You must remember that the Union saved Scotland.
Scotland was bankrupt and the English opened us up to
their American and Canadian markets, from which we just
flowered."

*

"The desire to be a politician should bar you for life from ever becoming one."

*

"Don't vote. It just encourages them.... "

*

I don't want to influence anybody so I shut up. I think the Scots will come to a good conclusion in the referendum. They'll get what they deserve."

*

"Scots are very capable of making up their mind without my tuppence worth."

*

He told the BBC:

"There's a thing I was always saying when I was asked about nationalism: I've never been a nationalist and I've never been a patriot. I've always remembered that I have a lot more in common with a welder from Liverpool than I do with someone with an agricultural background from the Highlands, although I do love them, I love Scotland and all its different faces. That's why this referendum thing is so difficult, it's a morass that I care not to dip my toe into."

*

About whether or not he would vote in the referendum on Scottish independence:

"I'm not going to vote. I won't be there, I'll be in New Zealand."

*

On the subject of Scottish independence in an interview with the Radio Times:

"I think it's time for people to get together, not split apart. The more people stay together, the happier they'll be."

DAVE FARNHAM

WHAT HE DISLIKES

"When people say "Oh you just want to have your cake and eat it too". F***ing right! What good is a cake if you can't eat it?"

*

"I f***ing hate going on holiday anywhere but in my own home. My idea of a nice break is lying in bed being brought cups of tea while watching football, episodes of Law & Order (1990) or one of those reality shows set in a prison. And it f***ing terrifies me to be somewhere where Pamela Stephenson's going to be lurking about waiting to guilt-trip me into going on a walk to Japanese gardens, sampling vanilla tea or trying to stay upright on a contraption that doesn't know if it's a kite or a surfboard. Wild horses couldn't persuade me. If she'd had her way, we'd start the day with an hour of power yoga on the shore, followed by a gluten-free breakfast, a scuba dive to see enormous, bitey things, then a tanning session on the beach where the combination of sunscreen and sand turns you into a giant schnitzel. After lunch there'd be kayaking to a deserted island, then a candlelit dinner in some exotic outdoor location where small bitey things make you even more miserable than the big ones."

*

"People who announce they are going to the toilet. Thanks that's an image I really didn't need."

*

"Jazz makes me want to vomit!"

*

"People who point at their wrist while asking for the time... I know where my watch is pal, where the f*** is yours? Do I point at my crotch when I ask where the toilet is?"

*

"When you're eating something and someone asks 'Is that nice?' No it's really revolting - I always eat stuff I hate."

*

"I f***ing hate sand."

*

"People who are willing to get off their arse to search the entire room for the TV remote because they refuse to walk to the TV and change the channel manually."

*

"I loathe hecklers. I haven't got a good syllable to say. When you come out of the club circuit and into the concert hall, they should be gone. There's an element of manners that should tell you that the ticket is dear and it's a different venue."

*

"People who ask 'Can I ask you a question?'. Didn't really give me a choice there, did you sunshine?"

*

"Toblerones! It's impossible to eat a f***ing Toblerone without hurting yourself!"

*

"People who say things like "My eyes aren't what they used to be." So what did they used to be? Ears? Wellington boots?"

*

"When you involved in an accident and someone asks 'Are you alright?' Yes fine thanks, I'll just pick up my limbs and be off."

*

"When people say while watching a film 'Did you see that?' No tosser, I paid 10 quid to come to the cinema and stare at the f***ing floor."

*

"When you are waiting for the bus and someone asks, 'Has the bus come yet?' If the bus came would I be standing here, Knobhead?"

*

"When people say 'It's always the last place you look'. Of course it is. Why the f*** would you keep looking after you've found it? Do People do this? Who and where are they?"

*

"I hate my country for the way it holds people back, tells them they're not good enough. I hate the tabloid press for what it does to people. Never letting them be intelligent."

*

"When something is 'new and improved!' Which is it? If it's new, then there has never been anything before it. If it's an improvement, then there must have been something before it."

*

"McDonalds staff who pretend they don't understand you unless you insert the 'Mc' before the item you are ordering... It has to be a McChicken Burger, just a Chicken Burger gets blank looks. Well I'll have a McStraw and jam it in your McEyes you f***ing McTosser."

DAVE FARNHAM

ASSORTED ONE-LINERS

"I don't know why I should have to learn Algebra... I'm never likely to go there."

*

"Did your mother never tell you not to drink on an empty head?"

*

"My parents used to take me to the pet department and tell me it was a zoo."

*

"Who discovered we could get milk from cows, and what

did he THINK he was doing at the time?"

*

"Don't buy one of those baby intercoms. Babies pretend to be dead. They're bastards, and they do it on purpose. "

*

"Never trust a man, who when left alone with a tea cosy... doesn't try it on."

*

"Reports of my demise have been greatly exaggerated."

*

"Oh, I've had a lot of the finger-up-the-bum. My doctor says, 'Pick a finger!' He's lovely. 'I'll have the signet ring please, but don't tell me what's written on it...'"

*

"My advice to you, if you want to lose a bit of weight: don't eat anything that comes in a bucket. Buckets are the kitchen utensils of the farmyard."

*

About his friendship with Princess Anne:

"I'm not going to throw away the hand of friendship to suit 100 Trotskyites in Glasgow."

*

The joke about a man who, having killed his wife, buried her in his back garden:

"His mate asks him, 'What did you leave her bum sticking out for?' He says 'I need somewhere to park my bike'."

*

"When I was twelve we went to Aberdeen from Glasgow on a school trip. It was called fresh air fortnight."

*

"All of my other hair just grows at the normal speed and I'm grateful to have some. But my nose hair?"

"I used to trim it once every 14 years or something but now it's three times a week."

*

Billy Connolly stopped taking medication for Parkinson's disease because of its damaging side effects which he says are:

"An overriding interest in sex and gambling."

"So if you see somebody in Las Vegas with an erection, he's probably got Parkinson's." He joked.

*

"My definition of an intellectual is someone who can listen to the William Tell Overture without thinking of the Lone Ranger."

WHAT OTHERS HAVE SAID ABOUT HIM

Pamela Stephenson, his wife, spoke about about Billy's health, August 2014:

"He's been ill and it was a huge shock to him – you know, for somebody who's been healthy his whole life to suddenly hear he has two major problems in a week.

"But, thank God, his Parkinson's is so mild he will never really have the kind of symptoms that many people associate with Parkinson's, as far as we know.

"What has happened is, he has probably had it for 10 years so it's very slowly progressing, thank God. There are different strains of Parkinson's that I am learning about.

"One is never sure about the course but he's doing incredibly well, there's no problem with his memory or anything like that. He doesn't need Parkinson's medication; it's too mild for that.

"I haven't noticed his hand shaking for many, many years now. I used to think he was playing the banjo a bit too much.

"Billy's one of these people who doesn't like going to the doctor so of course he was going to hear some bad news when he went after a while.

"But he's his curmudgeonly, loveable self and dealt with it the way that you would imagine he'd deal with it.

"He's had an operation for his cancer and is doing really well; he had a check-up recently and he's fine."

*

Billy's spokeswoman said, in September 2013 (about his diagnosis of Parkinson's disease):

"Billy has been assured by experts that the findings will in no way inhibit or affect his ability to work, and he will start filming a TV series in the near future, as well as undertaking an extensive theatrical tour of New Zealand in the new year."

*

Tom Harris, Labour MP for Glasgow South, described Billy Connolly as a:

"100 per cent Scottish hero."

He also said: "There is going to be this referendum but

those of us who want to be part of the UK have no organisation and no figurehead. Billy might say no but we need to ask him."

*

Eddie Izzard, comedian, said:

"Billy Connolly is the Moses of comedy who had Ten Commandments - each one being 'Thou shalt be very f***ing funny.'

"He helped stand-ups in the UK and Ireland find their own voice, as opposed to being totally influenced by American comics. He was about 10 to 15 years ahead of the scene in the UK. He influenced me hugely and I loved both his style of chatting personally to 2,000 people and of acting out scenes from stories.

"He was the first alternative stand-up comedian before there was a 'scene'. There was no one like him. He was playing characters on stage, ad-libbing and changing his material every time you saw him.

"I remember falling about on the floor watching Billy doing 'the incontinence knickers' sketch. It was part of a larger piece about Sunday newspapers and the weird adverts they run for useless items. When he applied the idea of incontinence knickers to a 'trendy guy', and then mimed him tying drawstrings around the legs of the knickers, it became absolutely killingly funny".

*

Fiona Allen, comedienne & actress, said of him:

"I remember watching Billy Connolly as a kid, and being totally bemused by his clothes and hair - I thought he was a mime artist or something.

"I loved his sketch about somebody knitting a balaclava for him, and him squinting because the eyeholes were in the wrong place! I laughed out loud and it made my belly ache.

"I was once introduced to him by a very boring guy at a party in Los Angeles. I never actually spoke to Billy but was lumbered all night with the boring guy. I was really disappointed.

"I'm not a believer in people standing up on stage and copying other people and, anyway, nobody could ever imitate Billy Connolly. Despite his dreadful dress sense, he is brilliantly funny."

*

Patrick Kielty, Irish comedian, said:

"When I was 14 or 15 my dad and I listened to a tape of Billy Connolly and for the first time we both actually got the same joke. The sketch was about how 'women demand things - more of this and not half as much of that - and whenever you've met all their demands they'll f***ing run away, so stay awake!' Me and dad found this so hilarious that the swearing was overlooked. Connolly has that ability to swear in a very ingratiating way - it's never aggressive and always done with a twinkle in his eye.

"Whereas lots of comedians go out on stage with set material and then go off on a tangent from time to time, Billy has a back catalogue so vast and a memory so good that he can be different every night.

"But it's his storytelling that places him above all other comedians. Connolly is not afraid to do the old-fashioned jokes sometimes, but he'll tell it like it's some personal life experience of his. I've seen him live a few times and remain in awe of him.

"He taught me that you can say literally anything you want to so long as you smile."

*

ITV's Jo Clinton-Davis said:

"Billy Connolly's a big fan of life, he's effervescent, energised and inspired by it, but he's also genuinely fascinated by the way we as humans treat death, a subject that is quite literally the ultimate universal experience yet so often avoided."

*

Comedian Jack Dee's, comments about him:

"Billy is that very rare person who, on stage, can create an atmosphere of laughter around him. He has a complete honesty about him and a fluency in comedy that makes the audience believe that he can translate anything into laughter for them. The more comedians you see the more you understand what a rare gift that is.

"Most British comedians take themselves terribly seriously, which suggests that they've failed to learn one of Connolly's greatest charms - his absolute refusal to do so.

"I remember seeing him on the Parkinson Show in the 70s and other odd clips from the telly of him in his banana shoes. I think his shampoo sketch was the most memorable: 'What's jojoba? Where I'm from that's the month before November.'

"I've never met Billy Connolly, but once, while shopping with my wife, I put aside a tie-dyed scarf that I liked. Then Connolly came in, tried on the scarf and said that he'd buy it. The shop owner said it was already spoken for and so Connolly left. Although it was far more expensive than I had thought, I bought it anyway because Billy Connolly had wanted it."

*

Eric Idle, comedian, wrote to Billy Connolly:

"You used to be a comedy god. Now you look like God."

*

Aberdeen Performing Arts press manager, Joyce Summers, says of Billy Connolly's tour beginning September 2014:

"We are thrilled to have Billy Connolly begin his latest tour with us at the Music Hall – although he is a global figure, we feel he is one of our own and the world did first see his big banana boots on our stage!

"When he last played the Music Hall five years ago, the tickets were instantly snapped by fans who burned up our phone lines and besieged the Music Hall, so we fully expect the 2600 up for grabs for the September nights to fly out the door on Friday."

*

Lindsay Scott, Age Scotland, said:

"We would love to have Billy as our ambassador. He's got the right frame of mind – he's a pretty good role model for a lot of older people.

"He's got the right idea – as soon as you start lapsing into the frame of mind, 'Oh, I'm old', then it doesn't stop you becoming older.

"Accept it and embrace it in a positive way but you should be still trying to do stuff. That includes, as he says, having sex.

"Any activity as you get old is good for you. Inactivity is the biggest enemy as you get older. It doesn't mean sitting down is bad for you. Billy is right – do things you enjoy."

Other Books by Dave Farnham

Snippets of Abraham Lincoln

Snippets of Benjamin Franklin

Snippets of Boris Johnson

Snippets of Donald J.Trump

Snippets of Fear

Snippets of Happiness

Snippets of Health

Snippets Of Jealousy

Snippets of Jeremy Kyle

Snippets of Joan Rivers

Snippets of Nigel Farage

Snippets of Oscar Wilde

Snippets of Marilyn Monroe

Snippets of Paul Gascoigne

Snippets of Richard Attenborough

Snippets of The Buddha

Snippets of Vladimir Putin

Snippets of Love

Snippets of Sex

Snippets of Success

Snippets of the British Royals

Gandhi's Teachings for Troubled Times